MW01119722

WRITERS REPUBLIC

Dandelions Are Me

KIKI LEIGH

WRITERS REPUBLIC L.L.C.
515 Summit Ave. Unit R1
Union City, NJ 07087, USA

Website: *www.writersrepublic.com*
Hotline: *1-877-656-6838*
Email: *info@writersrepublic.com*

Ordering Information:
Quantity sales. Special discounts are available on quantity purchases by corporations, associations, and others. For details, contact the publisher at the address above.

Library of Congress Control Number: 2021917969
ISBN-13:   978-1-63728-846-7   [Paperback Edition]
                  978-1-63728-847-4   [Digital Edition]

Rev. date: 09/17/2021

This book is dedicated to my family and Tanya.
And for people my poetry resonates with.

Contents

Dandelions Are Me

When I was off on one of my adventures during a manic spell, I smashed into a tree with my car trying to get away from this town from hell.

Somewhere, anywhere, far away. Someone above was looking down upon me to make sure that didn't happen because I was in no shape to be a runaway that day.

I biked around in the middle of the road and the stares I got, man they were bold. Truth be told it didn't bother me, nothing did when I was in that manic state. I was completely and utterly irate.

I rode by my friends house who was picking dandelions and weeds. After she saw me go by, she followed me.

Took me to the hospital for a psych evaluation because of the poor decisions I was making. Train wreck in the making, crazy lady on the loose with nothing to lose, although this wasn't true, it was to me at the time. The time when I couldn't make any sense out of anything going on in my mind.

Although feeling high on cloud nine and sublime, committing crimes, I had no intention to cause any harm, so this was a huge alert. Red flag, I was in trouble and I needed major help.

Thank God for my friend Tanya, mama bear, she took me there by the hair. Otherwise I would never be here, I would be 6 feet under covered in dirt. To you, a dandelion could be a small yellow weed. To me, a dandelion is symbolic and a big part of my story and history.

We are all perfectly imperfect. Nobody is perfect and that's a fact. We do our best to stay on track. All we can do is be our best selves, our most authentic version.

There's nothing wrong with being perfectly imperfect as it makes us all unique. I'm not even really sure what perfect is or even if it exists. I think our imperfections and flaws make us exactly who we are.

We make mistakes, we live, learn, laugh and love. Specially when life is so tough we learn as we go. We go with the flow, we try to inquire about things we don't know.

Embrace mistakes because there's lessons to be learned around every corner we turn and every endeavour we embrace, so if you believe you're perfect, you're wrong!

You are definitely worth it in every way and every day, so keep going strong, keep moving along, because life is unique in its own and we get the privilege to live it.

Why do we feel we have to do this and it's constantly undermining us and making us feel inadequate? We feel that everybody has to I guess, or there's something wrong with us or part of us that we stress about not being liked and we try so very hard but our soul pays the price.

We sacrifice our dignity and self worth just to please people we don't see or even know or care about but for some reason their opinions mean too much. Ultimately people's opinions don't matter but somehow put all this energy into being liked despite whom they are or where they're from it's all a game.

Is it everyone that feels the need to people please or just those that have insecurities? I don't know because I've always felt this way as long as I can remember, trying to prove myself to everyone is exhausting.

In all reality the only person you need to please is yourself, forget about the rest, and if you can live with just pleasing yourself then you know how to love YOU and it truly is enough.

Time to get better, sick of this weather. Dragging me down always wearing a frown. Time to reverse it up side down. Need to find me to be me and feel happy again. I'm tired of living in sin.

Time for a fresh start, time to start doing things right and follow my heart. I never understood the benefits of taking care of yourself. It's all about feeling well and my mental health.

Tired of feeling sluggish, it's all a bunch of rubbish. Tired of the self hate, it's time to celebrate all the small things that are great in life. It doesn't come without sacrifice. It's all about what you're willing to do to be the genuine you.

What I have and what I've done does not define me
Whom we surround ourselves with is what we will be
I have the urge to purge all the shit that doesn't matter
I get to decide whether I crack, crumble or shatter

It's all about building resilience and bouncing back
That doesn't happen if you have too much room for slack
It's all about making life decisions and getting off the fence
Especially in situations that make you feel tense

How many times have you questioned your worth?
How many times do you wish you could rebirth?
Change of social circle and status quo
And all people you know

It's not about quantity but quality
It's about the herbs and spices in life's recipe
Reality is perception based on beliefs
Perception can be changed by turning a new leaf

What you believe to be true
Has so much power over you
A million fish in the sea
So what's so special about me

You are the only you
You're the only one that can walk precisely in your shoes
The followed path is easy because it's beaten down

But your more likely to drown following a crowd
Time to take the path less taken
Because it's you who decides what footprints you're making
How many times do you search for approval
I'm telling you it's the root of all evil

Positive affirmation
Lessens limitations
Will unlock the inner strength
You kept in your emotional bank

Independence is a must
Dependence is a bust
To rely on anyone but yourself
Will rob you of your eternal wealth

I feel like the whole world is laughing at me waiting for me to fuck up so they can say I knew you would and point the finger. These are the thoughts that I have in my head and they linger.

Why cant I be strong and just truck along and have life easy and breezy for me? Although that's not my reality.

I do well for so long until I stumble, fall down, and hit the ground. Although I always get up after I crash.

It's like I've been hit by a Mac truck and always looking back. I should be looking forward but it's like I take two steps one way, two steps back to the other. Sometimes I seem put together but I'm not. I'm just stumbling around with a blindfold on hoping for the best.

Is life a test to see if you can make it, see if you can take it? All the battles, all the obstacles, all the uncertainty.

I want to live life and be free from the misery that I caused myself. I don't do it on purpose I swear some of it is eating at my mental health. I don't make the right decisions at the best of times but I try and I try and I cry and I cry. This time it's going to be different.

I'm going to do it the right way. I cannot continue this way. One more chance. I got this.

I have to for everyone and for everything this life brings.

I'm worth it. I must dig deeper than I've ever dug and rise above.

It's all about self love so I'm to love myself because it is you that has to be with you every day... So you have to be content with yourself in every way.

Good bye to self sabotage. Make the best of life, it doesn't come without sacrifice. That's okay I'll do it my way everyday because its my life. We only have one to live and that all I will give.

Jack

For many years I was an absent mom and I wasn't there for you, my beautiful son.

I had to go away and get myself healthy to be a better mom. My postpartum and bipolar depression kicked in with a vengeance. I felt completely and utterly empty.

But it was only me that could change this. I didn't feel good inside my mind, body, and soul. I wanted to run away and hide.

It was quite the roller coaster ride of emotions trying to heal myself to my very core, deep within. I missed a good portion of your early years. Still to this day I have a hard time with these memories of abandonment that I put you through. They are clear in my head and don't seem to want to fade away. They will always be here to stay.

Maybe less vivid in time. Today I'm happier than ever because you're in my life to stay. It took years for me to get this way. I had a lot of work to do and I had a lot to prove to myself and everybody else.

Although there are thoughts that haunt me, I have to remember it wasn't my fault it was my body's reaction and I needed to take action.

For years I didn't feel like your mother. It took time for others to step down the parent role they all took over in order for me to recover. I fought like hell to make you mine, and I would if I had to fight until the end of time.

If only I could press the rewind and start over to be there from the very beginning. Unfortunately I can't, I don't have a time machine to travel back in time and make you completely mine when you were just a little baby.

There are some things in life you can't control so there's no point of dwelling about it. It is what it is. It was what it was... But today is precious because now I know my son, who he is deep down inside, what makes him feel alive, what makes him feel happy inside.

He's one of my best friends and I will always be grateful that I had the opportunity to come back and be the mother I always knew I could be.

I love you Jack.

My Son

My son Jack Roberts has never been a brat. I know right, hard to believe and comprehend that this little boy is a godsend.

My son is literally like the sun. He rises and shines and sheds light in everybody's lives.

For my son I'd lay in front of a train and I'd jump in front of a crane to make sure that he lives the life best for him, and for that I would sacrifice a million times.

People should be scared this ain't no cub, this is a grown ass mama bear that absolutely has no care, if you hurt my boy it's me that will destroy.

You're my best friend, even so young you know when to talk and bite your tongue.

You're so mature, and an independent old soul.
You my son, have a heart of pure gold.

You're my soul and my heart, and nothing or nobody will ever keep us apart.

The only problem is you don't know how bright you shine, you're the brightest star on the darkest night.

You're one of a kind and the best part is you are mine.

Life for me has not been easy to say the least. Most of my life I've fought like hell within myself to be what seems to be society's normalcy.

Life is tough for someone with bipolar and addiction issues. It's like you're constantly swimming against the current, doing things you regret. Don't forget the everlasting anxiety and panic attacks that appear out of nowhere for no reason. Maybe subconsciously fighting a demon within me.

The roads I have taken were off the map. No wonder I always ended up with all the wrong people, all the wrong crowds, in all the wrong places, and seeing all the wrong faces.

I'm not a bad person don't get me wrong. I'm actually one of the kindest people and very strong. I've just made a lot of mistakes and poor decisions. To be honest with you I'm surprised I'm still living. Dangerous situations I've put myself in and didn't have proper judgement to know the difference.

I've been in a psychiatric ward for six months. That was tough, and I cried every night thinking this isn't right. To be locked away like some sort of animal that needs to be tamed.

I've also been to rehab cause I used to drink like a fish to abolish any memories and mental pain, from all the years of trauma and bad scenarios I've attracted.

Now I'm healing and doing my best, keeping strong, leaving the bottle alone. Taking my medication and trying to make the best out of my life situations.

35 years old, it's about time I get a break. I deserve it for all the shit I've endured. Time for ME to make positive changes, make the right decisions, and think things over. I'm done with this roller coaster, it's rickety and old and if I don't get off at soon it will break down, crumble, and fold.

I don't want this destiny for me. I want all my troubles to be history to make room for the new, improved me.

To be happy and to live in peace, to a lot of people that's life's foreign mystery. Some chase happiness in the dark, blindfolded, stumbling around with no intent and thinking they're completely content.

Most lie to themselves posting on social media, the Brady Bunch perfect picture, keeping up with the Jones's kind of idea.

The only people they're fooling is themselves because the rest of us all have it figured out.

The more you have to display what you've done that day, the more abundantly clear it is you're only chasing validation from people you don't know. It's just an act in a show.

If you're truly happy and fulfilled with abundance, you wouldn't feed in to all this garbage and bullshit. You carry on living your life without having to show or prove to anyone what you did that night.

Everyone deserves happiness but it doesn't come in a box wrapped up with a bow. It doesn't come from people and strangers you don't know, so if you can take the good out of every bad, thats a proud accomplishment that some people will never have.

Rather than happiness, I believe in happy moments and memories you build. I don't believe happiness is something that can be maintained 24-7 with all of life's obstacles and challenges.

So instead of wanting to find the key to happiness, practice gratitude. I believe this will better serve you.

It will prove that happiness does exist just not in constant motion. Kind of like the ocean it changes every day with it's waves and current. So happiness is there just stop looking for it.

Self Image

I look in the mirror and staring back at me is my own worst enemy.

Why is that the person I see? Why can't I see what others perceive and believe me to be?

I'm sure there are many that see themselves as their own best friend and are proud of their accomplishments to the very end. That I admire and want to acquire.

There's always room for improvement but nobody's perfect. I'm constantly inspiring to better myself and improve all areas and aspects of my life, including my own mental health.

To authentically love yourself through and through, faults and all, is life's biggest accomplishment and it's certainly something to be proud of and celebrate.

I've made a lot of mistakes in my life. I've broken a lot of promises and hurt a lot of people. Not intentionally or out of spite, just trying to figure out life's secret to feel completely happy and serene in life.

I believe if I continue to keep working away at myself, one day I will have the internal happiness and an abundance of wealth. It's not something that happens overnight. It takes a lot of work; it's like a job. But I'm willing to put in the work and wear it like a shirt.

Love me for me with zero apologies. That's how I see myself one day, hopefully in the near future. To be me and to be proud of who I see when I look in the mirror, and its abundantly clear that I love myself deep within.

Regardless of all my sins and mistakes, I want be able to forgive myself for the poor decisions I've made. New beginnings can start a new minute, moment, second, or day.

It's whenever you want to start to better your life. Mind you it doesn't come without sacrifice, but it's worth it because it's your life.

People believe that the great escape happens very far away, but in reality it happens anywhere and everywhere: The local bar, at campfires, or in the back of the car.

What wants to kill and destroy you yet you love and adore it? Let me give you a hint... It's everywhere you look tempting people all over the globe, anyone and everyone, even people we don't know.

I'm taking about drugs and alcohol. They want to kill and literally destroy us. Take our souls and minds. Yet, we get money out of our bank account to use it and abuse it and we choose to let it overtake our lives.

Most can't admit that they have a problem and believe if they use it, their problems will be solved. Overdosing has become a pandemic. It's a sad game to play, the game of chance with your own life just to throw it away.

Just to feel good once in a while or to feel nothing and empty inside. Temporary relief can turn into permanently deceased.

It's so dangerous these days. Once you try you're pulled in hook line, and sinker. Some try to get help, some sink deeper.

Some will stay in denial until the day is final. It's a sad disease, one of the mind, just like any other kind and it can get you at any time.

Drug addicts aren't bad people, they probably had unfortunate life events happen and turned to substances to save them from their mental pain or it would literally drive them insane. So that's why we use drugs to numb our brains so that everything feels okay.

Meriel

I met you when we were in the dark. I knew then what I know now you have the purest, kindest heart.

You were funny and shy, you dressed and acted so fly.

You were authentic and rad, you never let nobody bring you down

You had a cute little smile and smirk, you called anyone out if they were a jerk.

You treated everyone in the same genuine way, now you are at a peaceful lay.

I can't believe a beautiful soul like you had left us, but god must have needed a special angel to bless us.

I'll love you to the end. This heart will never mend, but memories of you I will place them together and remember forever.

You left a place in everyone's hearts. Meriel, until then we shall never part. Forever soul sisters.

Now wherever you are you can be free of the addiction mentality. You are a perfect angel in the heavens above, who all of us will forever love.

Manic

When I'm high without drugs I feel limitless
Supersonic, electric, spontaneous, carless

Ready to go, anywhere with anyone, even those I don't know
Its like I'm on stage
Lights, camera, action, I'm the star of the show

Euphoric, sublime, rejuvenated, happy, and full of life
Always on cloud nine feeling fine at all times

Living on the edge of my seat, never thinking repercussions and consequence
Not thinking anything through its like living in a circus

Just ready to have fun with the crew
I found that week
I herd them in like sheep

With my charm and fast wit
Keeps me interesting as shit

Presenting to the world a false identity
Don't forget its not my fault its my brains biological chemistry

Spending money I don't have
Run away and don't pay for a cab
Very manipulative and so convincing
A comedian and a liar
But her presence is FIRE!

But we all know this feeling eventually deteriorates
Sooner or later you drain all your dopamine and it doesn't last
Your going to lose control and inevitably crash

My brain is invaded by memories that devastate, thoughts swirl around and around like a carousel at a playground.

Continuously questioning, evaluating my own thoughts, actions, and behaviours. I think to myself please somebody help save her.

My brain feels like it weighs a ton of bricks. It's mentally, physically, and emotionally exhausting, no wonder I feel like shit!

It causes a lot of heartache, heartbreak, and pain. This could literally drive anyone insane.

I've been down some tough roads, paths throughout my life... Through a lot of shit. That my friend is legit.

I've been beaten, battered, and torn.
Clawed apart by a million thorns.
Crippling mental pain.
But I have no shame.
I've been thrown flat on my face... But I fight like hell to get back up! Those are the moments I need to embrace and celebrate.

I have a mental evil... Bipolar disorder lurks under the surface and lives within me.

It's not the same brain chemistry... Of that of a normal brain, that of an average Jane.

My meds keep me on an even keel, but the struggle is real and feels surreal.

Bipolar is a mystery, its all an experiment. I will forever be a guinea pig with the tweaks and adjustments. Bipolar will forever mark history.

It's no wonder I'm crippled with anxiety and feel tense. Oh and not to mention bipolar fog. Makes me feel dense, sad, scared, and confused.

The best part is I have to endure this mental battle all by myself, my compromised mental health.

Every bipolar diagnosis is different so I can't help but to feel indifferent.

One day... I'm telling you, I will shine!! Like a bright star on a dark clear night, let me tell you it doesn't come without sacrifice.

Even though it will always be a lifetime battle, I will never back down, I will never crack, crumble, or shatter.

I will prevail and live to tell the tale.

I'm not a survivor... I'm a warrior !!!!

Some believe that things in life happen by chance, others believe things happen to them. I believe things happen for you. Life is sort of like flying a kite, you never know what direction it will flow. It's all unknown until you let the rope go.

It's all about taking chances. We only have one life to live so it's you that gets to decide how much you wanna give. Give it your all or half-assed. Go through the motions or go leaps and bounds, climb mountains and cross oceans.

I'm not here to say that any of these ways are right or wrong to each their own. Whatever makes you happy, that's the key.

Whatever life you live, simple or extravagant, it's yours to decide. That's the beauty of it, that we have choices. Some we make are excellent, some we make are absurd. That's the nature of the game.

We all learn this way through the good and bad decisions. It changes things for us. Like our perception and vision, maybe to rethink our path and go a different route. There's always obstacles, but I'd like to think of obstacles like stepping stones to our future success.

One door closes, another opens. If you hit rock bottom, the best part is the only way to go is up. So believe in yourself and always reach for the stars. Shoot, even reach for Mars because your dreams are not far away.

Your dreams can be right under your nose you just need to know how to seize the opportunities, whatever they may be. You never know what you're capable of until you take a leap of faith and believe in yourself. The most important thing is it doesn't matter what anyone else thinks, it's your life so live it the way you see fit.

I've been through some tough shit
And yes my friend thats legit

I've been beaten battered and torn
Clawed apart by a million thorns

It's not that easy being me
Does not matter my family tree
Or how I was raised

Its more then just environment and toxic people
Its all about my mental evil

Bipolar lives within me
Its not the same brain chemistry

Not that of a regular brain
It literally drives me insane
Just to be "normal"

The right meds keep me even and on keel but the
struggle is real
And it feels surreal

Most bipolar treatments are a mystery
Its all a experiment
And will forever mark history

I have to endure this myself
My comprised mental health

Every bipolar diagnosis is different
So I can't tell but to feel indifferent

So feeling very much alone in my own mind
One day I'm telling you I will shine

Even tho its a battle I never back down
I will never suffocate or drown

I'm not a survivor I'm a warrior !!!

My Gramma Faye

I have so many fond memories I love about you grandma Faye that are stuck in my head forever and will never fade away. I will never forget you, I will cherish you forever.

You made a mark in my heart and deep down in my soul. I know you're not far, you're not here in body, but your here in spirit and memory in our hearts.

I remember the Midland Mountain View Mall and the bumpy halls when you'd push us in the cart.

You always took us to Teddy's Diner for a fry and a drink and always brought us a special little treat.

I remember Camp Run-a-Muk and all the fun we had. My lovely grandmother, you never missed a beat.

You were always there as a guiding light throughout my life.
I remember your soft hands comforting me, rubbing my leg and holding my hand, telling me everything's going to be okay.

All the sleepovers and slumber parties were always so fun at your house. The time you shrieked at the trailer when you saw a mouse.

I never wanted to leave, you're place was such a ball. I still have the Christie doll you thought look like me. What a special memento and memory.

You always remember all our birthdays and showed us how you cared in so many different ways. I remember running away to your house but eventually I never got to stay. I always had to go back until the next time I ended up your way.

You were there through the good, the bad, and the ugly. Truly a gem, you are a beauty of a grandma and a person.

Nobody could replace you or fill your shoes. You were one of a kind and the best part is you were mine.

My grandma was the best lady around. Now and forever you're looking down on us, protecting us like you did when you were here on earth every day.

One of my best memories is the Robert Munch book you used to read us before bed. My version is... I'll love you forever, I'll like you for always. As long as I'm living my grandma you'll be.

We all love you and miss you.

These days sobriety is far-reaching. It is so socially acceptable it's almost unacceptable not to drink to fit in when socializing. Why is drinking such an 'in' thing? Is it because it loosens our tongues and it's easier that way? Or is it an escape from reality because we can't stand the current situation we are facing?

Most people drink too much but that's a subject they don't want to touch. They just deny themselves, they don't have to feel the feels and nothing is a big deal all is forgiven and forgotten when you drink the bottle to the bottom.

Basically it's poison we drink so we don't have to think or we can blame our poor decision making on the substances we are taking. In fact we know very clear what we're doing, it becomes hard for ourselves to look at the mirror. Some people suffer more than others, some can't control their substance abuse. Some people use different things for different reasons but it leaves a lesion, like a scar on your heart that lurks under the surface.

We wake up and never feel good opposed to when we're sober, although we forget that feeling it becomes a never ending spiral and we keep doing it blindly in denial. Most chase the buzz, the fuzzy feeling in your head and if you use it too much it's becomes a crutch. Without it you won't be sturdy enough, eventually you crash. That's when you hit rock bottom and it becomes a big problem.

So although you think you need booze to have a good time, that just means you're not happy with yourself or anybody else. Do you have to use to pretend you feel okay and at the end of the day you know that it's not that way?

When you set goals and you chase dreams that are big, good things will come from them.

Of course you have your sceptics that don't believe in you and think it's a pipe dream and there's no point to even follow through.

They can be the closest to you strangers friends but most don't believe in you. The problem with that is they only believe what they see to be true. Whatever happened to blind faith?

It doesn't matter what you say or what you do, though you don't have to prove anything to anybody that you know except for you. That's really the only person that you need to impress.

Forget about validation, forget about trying to convince people that you have something in the making. It's your creation, it's your invention, and it's your life for the taking.

So just do you, do what you gotta do and believe in yourself, believe in your achievements, believe in your creativity and authenticity. There's nothing that you cannot acquire or aspire to be.

If you keep trying and never give up, failure is steps to success. You may not get it the first time but you have the rest of your life, so just be patient and give yourself some grace and the rest will all fall into place.

Have you ever had bipolar plus borderline personality disorder?

Don't forget addiction issues along with all that judgement and the never ending tissues.

You get all the right pills, you do all the right drills.
It doesn't seem to matter, eventually it all just shatters.

My mind doesn't cooperate on a regular day, it's set to a different pace. Its not enough that I'm chemically entwined, with no rewind.

Always the wrong combination. No medication... Meditation... Relaxation... Can rewire my brain... From this mental pain.

My Little Secret

I have a secret I want to share but let's be aware it's something I'm not proud of. It's something I am most definitely ashamed of.

I never thought this would happen to me. I thought that I was smarter than this. I never thought it would happen to me but low and behold it did and I'm not looking for empathy.

Let's start from the beginning. That's usually the best place to start. I take medication every day and every night. It's for the bipolar illness that I have to fight.

For years I had a drinking problem. I thought alcohol would solve all my issues. Maybe not solve them but definitely numb them post-trauma. So here's the dilemma, I fell off the wagon and drank a few full flagons then got behind the wheel of my car. I didn't even get very far and I smashed into two cars. Fractured my ribs thankfully everyone lived.

I wish it wasn't true, the story I'm telling you, I'm so ashamed and I'm the only one to blame. Now I have to lay in the bed that I made and pay the consequences that come my way. Every time I think about what I did that day it makes me think twice about about life and sobriety. Things could've definitely been worse.

So now I have to go through the legal system and pray that I don't get a harsh penalty, but every time I think about that day I pray and I thank God I'm still here to tell the tale.

I'm not a bad person. I made a stupid decision and now I have to live with that. If anything it's taught me a very important lesson: I can never drink, not even just one.

Today is your special day to celebrate you in each and every way. There are so many things to say about you mom, because to me you are the bomb!!

When I was growing up young, dumb, and naive, the way I perceived you was way off course... I didn't realize or recognize all you did for me. It was as if I was blindfolded and could not see.

I took everything you did for granted I just thought you're a mom and its your obligation to go above and beyond.

Now that I'm grown and have two kids of my own, I know you are and have always been a SUPER MOM!

Taking care of all those daycare kids plus four of your own, to make sure we had everything we needed and a beautiful place to call home.

You worked your ass off and sacrificed a lot for us just to make sure we were all happy.

Your the strongest women I know.
Tough as nails, with a heart made of gold.

You are beautiful inside and out...
I still don't know how you did what you did and continue to do what you do and for that, I want you to know that I'm proud of you, I love you and adore you.

So thank you so much for being the best mom a girl could ask for. I could not ask for anything more. You do so much for me and my family and have this energy about you that makes people happy and smile.

I love you from the bottom of my heart and I simply feel blessed.

Mom, you are the BEST!

Toxic relationships; If the relations make you sick and feel like shit, you are definitely in a toxic environment. Your constantly feel belittled and inadequate.

Most don't know we are in them because we've become accustomed to being used and abused that we don't even realize that we are being deceived and manipulated. We think it's normal to be going through all this drama and turmoil. But that's not the case at all.

Sometimes it's easier looking from the outside in then the inside out to see what your relationship is all about. Once you gain some confidence and strength and see through a different lens it's only then you can free from the chains and from the mental games that hold you back.

When you love yourself authentically and truly for who you are you can reach for the stars. True friends will come your way and true friends will stay and you won't feel hurt and betrayed.

Who am I, where do I belong.
This road I'm on is too windy and I don't feel strong.
I used to think things were going good.
I thought I've done all that I could.
My thoughts are dark and scary.
These burdens I have to carry.

I want to escape from my own head.
This negative self image and thoughts I need to shed.
Please give me the courage and strength.
I feel like I'm walking the plank.
I have no energy and don't feel happy inside.
I miss when I used to feel alive and walked with pride.

I need to make changes, I know this.
But it's so hard when you constantly feel like shit.
Like you've been run over too many times.
All I wanna do is run away and hide.
Please tell me things will soon change.
But the sad part is I'm the only one to blame.

Purpose

We all have a purpose in this life but what it is we do not know. Although some do find our purpose early in life, some of us fall down hit the ground searching.

We all have talent, strength, and wisdom that we could share with the world. Some of us just don't know which avenue to take, which road to turn.

We constantly compare our lives to others like our brothers, sisters and friends. I often wonder if we are where we should be. The answer to that question is you are where you are and you are where you should be, although you may feel as though it's a mystery.

People believe you need to be rich and wealthy to be successful, but in reality that is not true. Success is anything you want it to be; success is in you. So I don't search for clues, it will all come at the right time and place just follow and have some faith.

Inadequate

Have you ever felt inadequate, no matter what you do, no matter what you say, accomplish, or acquire? Anything and everything you do, it's never enough to admire.

Do you try so hard to impress or do you love to get some sort of validation or praise? You can't stop, it's like a drug. You chase it every day but that feeling of inadequacy never goes away.

It's like an addiction, always searching for approval.

I'm learning that approval comes from within, not from others or strangers or loved ones.

I mean it wouldn't hurt to be held on a pedestal and be praised and thought of every day.

It hurts more when you open the door and there's nobody or nothing there for you to share your proudest moments with.

So just know that all the validation in the universe comes from you.

When you believe this to be true, nothing or nobody has any power over you.

You are at peace with yourself, you are proud of your accomplishments, you are proud of yourself and in the end that's more than a whole bunch of financial wealth.

So remember just being you is more than enough. Even when times are tough, never give up.

Missing Me

Missing me like crazy
Feeling so tired and lazy
Held back and withdrawn
Feeling like a horrible mom
Need to get back to myself
Certain things I can't help
Certain things I can
I have a plan

To utilize all my sources
Take some courses
Work hard play less
Be nothing but the best
Take my words into action
Positive law of attraction

Conquer all my fears and anxiety
By facing them in my current reality
Eat good, feel great
To my lover a good teammate
Get myself up and moving
Turn my thinking around so I'm not losing
Read more, learn more
Go completely hardcore

Stop drinking
Get thinking
So much that life has to give
So much life I have left to live
Have to up my standards

I deserve better
Stop complaining about weather
And small insignificant things
Time to grow my wings
Fly as high as I can
Yep, that's my plan

Powerless

Why is it I feel that I'm always having to fight hard for the things I need and want, and what I want is certainly not a lot.

The struggle I go through each day is real. I feel uneven and off keel.

 I need all my strength to heal all the wounds I have made. Sometimes I'm brave, other times I want to cave.

It seems to be a pattern of mine, sometimes I shine bright like a star. Sometimes those stars are way too far for me to reach.

Theres so many things I want to achieve, accomplish and acquire. So many people I admire. I admire those the most that have a consistent pace in their daily lives. I admire those that always seem to thrive.

Can I be that person one day? I know I want it bad enough but my positive outlook doesn't always stay that way.

I have so many demons I feel I'm always slaying. I want to be making a better impression on this place we call earth. I want to have abundance and self worth.

Can I do these things others do? Can I accomplish anything I put my mind to?

Something always seems to get in my way. Maybe its me, myself and the girl I see in the mirror everyday. Whatever it may be I will continue to strive for the stars. Even if they are so very far.

One day I will get there.
One day.

Changing

I'm changing my life, like it or not
I'm changing my life, rewriting the plot
I'm changing my life, calling all the shots
I'm seeing through a different lens
My body needs a spiritual cleanse
I know I can do this

No more playing the victim and self sabotage
I'm not just improving I'm reinventing myself
I'm going to have the best life and mental health
Going to make a vision board
The old me I'm pulling the cord
She's dead to me

She had eyes but couldn't see
Going through life wanting more without putting in the
time
This girl is ready to shine
In all aspects and areas
She finally has clarity

Take time to get there, progress not perfection
She realizes this world is hers for the taking
She accepted she deserved the life she had
She accepted that she should be a failure and sad
You were put on this life for a reason
Not just for a shitty time and season
Happiness is the world's best gift
All she can do is make the shift

She will get everything she's ever desired and more
It's all about changing herself to the very core
She will stop being broken, pick those pieces up and
use them as a token

Life does not come without sacrifice
Sacrifice is the name of the game it doesn't come without
pain
Pain and failure are footsteps to pride and success
You will never settle for anything less
Then what you are and want to be
Put that on your horizon and make tomorrow history